A New Beginning:
Fighting to get back up on
SKIS

A New Beginning:
Fighting to get back up on
SKIS

AUBRIE MINDOCK

iUniverse, Inc.
Bloomington

A NEW BEGINNING:
FIGHTING TO GET BACK UP ON SKIS

iUniverse books may be ordered through booksellers or by contacting:

iUniverse
1663 Liberty Drive
Bloomington, IN 47403
www.iuniverse.com
1-800-Authors (1-800-288-4677)

Because of the dynamic nature of the Internet, any web addresses or links contained in this book may have changed since publication and may no longer be valid. The views expressed in this work are solely those of the author and do not necessarily reflect the views of the publisher, and the publisher hereby disclaims any responsibility for them.

Any people depicted in stock imagery provided by Thinkstock are models, and such images are being used for illustrative purposes only.
Certain stock imagery © Thinkstock.

ISBN: 978-1-4620-5050-5 (sc)
ISBN: 978-1-4620-5049-9 (hc)
ISBN: 978-1-4620-5117-5 (ebk)

Printed in the United States of America

iUniverse rev. date: 08/24/2011

Forward

To be honest, I never thought that I could write a book, especially about myself. It was actually difficult to start my story but I saw something that would be inspiring to others. For me, being able to inspire others is something that I have always dreamed of doing.

Before I tell you about my accident, I am going to introduce myself. My name is Aubrie Mindock. I am an 18 year old female who loves sports, especially skiing. I have a great family who inspires me to do my best with whatever it may be.

In some ways, I am just an ordinary 18 year old girl, and in other ways, I am different from most 18 year olds. One way that I am different is when I was 15 years old I was in a bad skiing accident. The accident almost took away my life and my ski racing. I had to do a lot to get myself back on the slopes.

I never thought that I would be able to return to racing after the accident. The thought of having to quit and give up everything that I had worked so hard for made me upset. I was determined to get back up on the race course. It wasn't going to be easy but I was ready to give it everything I had.

When I was lying in the hospital bed after sugary I made a promise to myself. That promise was that I would try my hardest to get back up on skies but also try my hardest with everything I do in my life. My journey back wasn't easy but it was worth it.

When I got back up I was stronger and more prepared than ever. Through hard work I was able to race once again. I had proven to myself and my family that I could do it. The lesson I learned during those months was to never give up no matter how hard the goal may be.

I had always believed in trying my hardest and always doing the best you can in life. I have always been a hard worker and not one to complain or quit. At an early age my parents, especially my dad, told me that in order to succeed in life you must never give up and you should always work hard.

If someone had told me that I was going to have a bad accident, almost die and lose the sport I loved I wouldn't have believed them. At the age of 15 you do not think about bad things happening to you.

You think that you are invincible and that nothing comes hard. After the accident I learned the truth.

Everyone has hardships and tough times. What makes a person stand out is what they decide to do during their hard times. When you pull yourself together and work for what you want you will be rewarded in the end with your goal.

Even today I have to live with bad pain in my ribs and lung. My knee still hurts from time to time too. Every day is a battle to stay strong. It is not always easy. A lot of the time I have to work through pain, even when I am relaxing. I do deep breathing exercises to get me through the painful times. Even though I will have lifetime difficulties as a result from this accident I am just glad that I got my racing back and that I am able to live a normal life again.

While reading my story I do not want you to feel sorry for me. I do not want you to think that my life is ruined because of what happened. In fact I am glad that the accident happened. If the accident didn't happen then I would never have learned the things about myself and my life. Also, this story does not have an ending. I am still living and I am excited for the many new experiences and challenges that lay ahead of me.

After my accident I was told that I could never race again by friends and family. The people I knew and loved wanted me to return to recreation skiing. I did not want that. Skiing competitive is what I love to do. Having to quit racing was something that I was not going to give up on. I did everything that I could possibly do to get back up.

No one was going to tell me what I could and could not do. I was not going to let someone tell me that I was not strong enough to get back up. I was going to let myself decide whether or not I was strong enough and when the right time for me to get back up was. It was my decision and no one else's.

Before you read my story I just want you to understand that it is hard for me to write about myself. I am writing because I think that by reading my story you will find hope and go for your dreams. Life has little lessons every day. Sometimes you can figure them out right away and sometimes you have to dig a little deeper. The lesson I learned the day of my accident is life is short. I also learned that Life is full of wonder and hardships. I took my ski accident and turned it into a lesson. It only made me stronger.

Life before the accident

I can't remember a time when I was not skiing. My dad had taught me to ski at the age of two in my back yard. My dad bought me a pair of little white skies and white boots. Every morning I would wake up, attempt putting my ski clothes on, run down to my dad's room and jump on my dad's bed until he woke up. I loved skiing. It was my favorite thing to do in the whole wide world. My dad didn't know what he was getting himself into the day he taught me to ski.

Almost every day when I was two, my dad would take me skiing. I thought I was so cool because I got to learn before my little brother Austin. Life does not get much better than being able to ski every day when you are little. It is a kids dream come true.

A few years later, when I was about 12, I got into freestyle skiing (bumps and jumps). My mom and dad decided that it was time for Austin and me to start getting competitive. They put us on Team Summit at Copper Mountain Resort. I was so excited to finally be on a team and could not wait until my first day. During my time on Team Summit I learned many new tricks off jumps and skied bumps until my legs could not take anymore. It was the life. I also made many new friends. Team Summit did not last long though, for I had racing on my brain.

One year I got tired of freestyle and wanted to go to racing. I had raced many times and thought it was more fun because I could go much faster. When I was 15 (the year of my accident) my dad found a new team called Quantum Sports Club. Quantum is the Breckenridge ski team. Immediately I started making new friends and having a blast out there. Being on Quantum was the best time of my life. My coaches quickly taught me how to improve my technique and increase my speed. Racing soon became my passion. If I wasn't racing I was training. I loved it and to this day still do.

I was never afraid of speed or nasty spills. When it came to speed fear was not a factor for me. The faster I went the happier I was. I loved going 70 miles per hour on skies. When I would fall I would get right back up and speed again.

I took some nasty spills and still do to this day. The thing is you cannot allow fear of falling affect you. When you fall you just shake it off like it was nothing. Sometimes, if a fall is bad enough, you are not able to just shake it off. When I had my accident it was impossible to shake off the injury.

For me I just love being on the mountain. Every time I was on the mountain I felt like I was in heaven. There isn't a better feeling than heaven. I would always have a smile on my face, even if I wasn't skiing well that day. How could you not have a smile on your face? Once I was on the mountain it was almost impossible to get me off. What can you say, I loved it.

Every day around 4:00 I would be forced by the ski patrol to leave the mountain, for I was always the last one off. That was ok. I didn't mind too much. The reason I did not mind is because in my back yard in Breckenridge we have a steep hill. The hill is actually a ski trail that we call ski in ski out. I can ski down that hill all night if I want to because the hill never closes. I also enjoy getting my flying saucer out and going down the hill standing on it. I don't last long while standing but it is a blast to do anyway.

I trained hard every day and I still do. My regular work out routine was and still is running four to six miles almost every day, weight training every other day, stretching, and eating only organic foods. I do this because I know that it will make me stronger and healthier for the up coming season. Sometimes, I feel like I don't want to lift weights, or run. When I feel like that, I remind myself of how far I have come, and that motivates me. It took a lot of work for me to come back and get this far. I will never give up, or quit.

By the end of the ski season I found myself fighting not only for my life but also for my dreams and the sport I loved. I would learn that life has many obstacles. It wouldn't be easy to overcome this one but I knew that if I wanted to ski again then I would have to give it 110 percent. I was ready to take this challenge and overcome it. The road ahead was going to be rough but I was ready to fight to get back up.

Picture

This was taken the year after I learned to ski. I was about three years old and defiantly up to something.

Racing Pictures

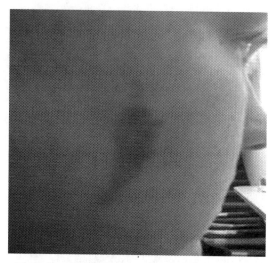

Frostbite: 18 years old. I've had worse!

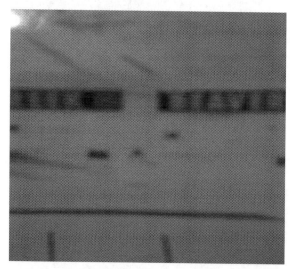

I am the little black dot. This was a Beaver Creek Giant
Slalom race where I placed 4th.
I was about 16 years old.

Me at 19 years old: At Purgatory just out with friends
for a fun day on the slopes.

Me at 15: A few days before the accident

I had just finished a race and was stoked because I had placed first. The trophy is pretty awesome that I won!

Day of the Accident

It was a beautiful April 11th day. It had snowed several inches the night before. The sun was shining brightly in the blue sky. There was not a cloud for miles. Austin and I had decided to ditch training that day. I never ditch training unless there is new snow or I am sick. I was definitely not sick.

Austin and I got our ski clothes on and quickly ate breakfast. We then walked to the lift. We got to the chair around 7:45. The chair does not open until 8:15. That gave us plenty of time to do our warm up which consists of running up and down the hill ten times, swinging our legs back and forth, doing squats, running in a figure 8 for several minutes and stretching (my favorite). When we finished our warm up it was time for the lift to open. Of course we were the first ones on.

Finally we got off the lift. The ride seemed to take forever, for I was anxious to get on the snow. Austin decided that he wanted to ski the steep bowls and I was not going to argue with that, epically with all the new, fresh snow.

Getting to the steep stuff is a little difficult. After a long hike we finally made our way to the T-bar. The T-bar looks like an upside down T. When riding it you have to stand. If you sit you will fall off.

When we got off we made our way to the Horseshow Bowl. The bowl is really steep and has cliffs, (or rock jumps) that you can jump off of. Skiing the bowl was great. The fresh snow was terrific. It was like skiing on a cloud.

Austin and I skied the bowls all day. We did not even take time to stop for lunch. Later on that afternoon we had decided to take a break from the bowls and ski the bumps. The bumps were awesome as well. They were steep and powdery, just the way we like them. I was also able to get some air off the bigger bumps. Skiing the bumps made me miss my freestyle days a little.

After about five hours of skiing bumps, we got a little tired. We had been skiing for about six hour's non stop. Austin and I decided to ski the groomed runs for a little while, and take it easier. What a blast we had. It was the best day of my life so far. I didn't want the day to end yet. It was now about 3:50. The lifts close at 4:00. Austin and I had to make a decision. We had to decide whether or not to take another run. We both knew that if we missed the lift it would be a long walk home in ski boots. We didn't mind the walk. Missing the lift was worth one more run.

We took the Colorado super chair up to the top. When we got off, it was 3:55. The run to the bottom takes about 2 minutes. We decided not to call it a day, and to take one last run before going home. That last run was one run I will never forget.

The Accident

I was skiing fast. I don't know how fast but it was fast. I love speed and my motto is the faster the better. Austin was close behind me. As I started to get close to the bottom of the run I could see the chair. I knew that I was going to make the lift. I also knew that the day was over, or so I thought.

As I got closer to the chair I decided to slow down. As I came up from my tuck my ski got caught in a rut and popped off, which is normal during a fall. I flipped into the air like a rag doll. When I landed my other ski popped off causing me to flip a second time. When I landed from my second flip my knee hit the binding of my ski. I went head over heels. As I was going head over heels my pole which did not slide off my wrist like it's supposed to stabbed me in the ribs. I suddenly felt several cracks in my rib cage but it did not hurt.

As I came to a stop I found myself lying on the snow. I was not breathing and I was spitting up blood. At first I thought the blood was coming from my mouth. I thought that I bit my lip or tongue. Then I started to realize that I was bleeding from my lung.

I was able to slowly roll to my knees. Once on my knees I started to feel weird. I hadn't had a single breath of air for almost a full minute. I started to feel like I was going to die. I was not afraid, nor was I ready.

I started to think about my family. I thought about my brother who was watching from below. I did not want him to see me die. I wanted him to know that I was not in pain. I remember looking at him and tried to smile. I tried to yell out to him that I would be alright but I could not talk. I kept trying to say something but I couldn't. I was desperately trying to tell my brother that I was not hurting, for there was no pain.

My mom also came to mind. She lost her first husband to a drunk driver a while back and it would be hard for her to lose a child too. I knew that I had to stay alive for her.

After I thought of my mom, my dad popped into my mind. I thought about the first time he taught me to ski. A smile came to my face when I thought about those little white skies. My dad and grandfather put a lot of effort into teaching me how to ski and it would be selfish of me to leave them behind. I then realized that he would be devastated if he lost his ski buddy.

After that thought, I started to feel dizzy. I could feel my eyes closing, for what I thought to be the last time. I then started to pray. I prayed that my family would be able to recover if they lost me and I prayed that I would be safe in Heaven.

Again, I thought of my mom. I prayed for her. She needed a prayer. Then I thought to myself, "No, I can't leave my mom. She needs me." At the moment I thought that I took my first breath of air. It felt so good to breathe again. My eyes fully opened. I do not know how long I had stopped breathing for. It is amazing that I was able to think of all of that stuff in a short amount of time. It is funny how when you get hurt you always think about your family no matter how old you are. You always want your parents to comfort you when you are in a sticky situation.

I think I was in shock and I did not know what to do from there so I started to get up. A man had gathered all of my stuff and brought it down to me. I have never had a fall that bad before. I got up and put my skies on. Somehow, I was able to ski the rest of the way down the mountain on one ski to the lift where Austin was waiting for me.

It was now past 4:00 but luckily the lift attendant had seen my fall. He kept the chair open a little longer. Before I got on the chair, the attendant asked me if I was ok. I told him that I was going to try to make it home. I knew that I was going to need patrol but I was trying to avoid them as much as possible.

The ride up the mountain was awful. I kept coughing, and blood kept coming up. I was afraid that I was going to stop breathing again. I prayed that I would make it up to the top where help was. I realized that I needed help and fast.

When we got off the lift I decided that I was going to ski to help. I could have laid back down on the snow and let help come to me but I decided not to. It was faster to ski to help. I told Austin that I was going to go to ski patrol (mountain paramedics). Austin and I both knew that I needed help badly.

I skied down a little ways to the patrol hut at the Vista Haus warming hut. I was hoping to see a ski patrol person outside but to my disappointment there were none so I was forced to walk inside to get help. As I was walking in I could feel a "crunch, crunch" in my knee. It did not hurt but I knew that it was not normal.

When I got inside my knee started to hurt a little. I looked down and saw that something was not right with it, for it did not look like a normal knee. I sat down in a chair outside of the patrol hut and waited for a person to come out. I knew that someone would come out eventually. They always come out to kick people off the mountain.

A few minutes later a patroller finally came out. I grabbed her attention by saying, "I need help." She did not hesitate to help me. I told her about my fall and that I did not know what my injuries were because I wasn't in pain. I told her that I had been coughing up blood. She told me to stay where I was and that she would help me. I watched her walk into her patrol area and a few seconds later a lot of patrol men were around me. It seemed like the entire patrol was swarming over me.

One person put an oxygen mask on me and another put a leg brace on me. The leg brace was heavy. I could not move my leg at all with it on. They then lifted me up and carried me outside. When we got outside there was a toboggan (a sled). The patrollers carefully put me on it and wrapped me up in warm blankets. They put my skies next to me.

In the sled I started to cry. I do not know why I was crying but I guess it was because I was relieved that I was getting help. The guys tried to calm me down by trying to make me laugh. I had to be calm for the ride down the mountain.

Finally, I was ready to start the long, slow ride down to the medical area. A female patroller grabbed the handle bars at the front of the sled. Before we started down the mountain she said to me, "If you need anything, then tell me and we will stop." She then pulled the sled and off we were. A man on a snowmobile followed close behind.

About half way down the mountain I started to feel like I was going to pass out. The guy on the snowmobile must have noticed because he yelled "stop." I remember stopping. I also remember saying a little prayer. Then everything went black.

When I woke up I was at the bottom of the mountain, lying on a bed. My boots were off. The woman was sitting next to me. She told me that they had gotten a hold of my dad and that I was going to go to the hospital. She also told me that my dad was already in the hospital for a broken finger. He fell earlier that morning skiing. I did not get to ski with him that day because he came out later on that morning.

I asked the lady who was going to take me to the hospital and she said an ambulance. I had never been in an ambulance before and I was a little scared. The lady told me that everything was going to be alright and the paramedics were going to take care of me. A few minutes later I heard sirens. They were loud and shrill. I was a little scared but I knew that I needed help.

The paramedics rushed in. They asked me many questions like, "How much pain are you in", and "How long ago did it happen". After they drilled me with questions they did some tests. One man took my pulse and the other man talked to patrol about my parents. The man who took my pulse turned to the other guy and said, "We have to go." Then they put me on a stretcher and covered me with a blanket. I never thought that I would be so ready to get off the mountain.

The ambulance ride felt long. It was only about a 10 minute ride but it felt longer. The only cool part was getting to run all the red lights and stop signs. The paramedic in the back with me kept talking to me and doing tests. I did not like the tests. I didn't understand why he had to do so many. I was glad when I finally got out of there.

The hospital was not much better. There were many doctors around me asking me many questions and doing many tests. I had to go in for X-rays and had to get scans and all kinds of weird stuff done. I wanted out real bad.

Finally I got a break. The doctors and nurses had left my room for a little while to look at my x-rays and test results. I got a little time to talk to my dad. My dad was real calm. We talked like there was nothing wrong. We did not even talk about my accident. I was glad to talk about something different.

My dad and I talked about the runs Austin and I skied. We laughed when we talked about both of getting hurt on the same day. Our time together was short. When the doctors came in, they told me what my injuries were.

I had serious injuries. My knee was broken. Also in my knee I had a torn meniscus, cart ledge, MCL, LCL, ACL, and a pad of fat was torn up. In my chest, I had a broken rib, and a badly bruised lung. My lung was bruised so badly that there was blood coming out of it. The doctors told me that my lung wasn't bleeding badly enough for emergency surgery but surgery on my knee would have to be delayed until my lung healed. I was relieved to hear that. My knee was put in a brace. I was glad that I did not need a cast.

I was scheduled for surgery a few weeks later. I wasn't looking forward to this recovery. I knew that I was going to need to stay positive if I was going to get through this.

Journal Entry

April 12th

Dear Diary,

Yesterday I was in a bad accident. I was flying down the mountain with Austin and I caught an edge and fell. I am no longer able to ski. No one knows if I will even be able to race again.

I really hope that I get better and can ski once more. I do not want to lose this sport. My dream is to be an Olympic athlete and I am not ready to give that up yet. I want to be on the U.S. Ski Team and compete in the Olympics. I want to win the gold.

My injuries are bad. My knee is broken and all torn up. My ribs are broken and my lung is really badly bruised. I was coughing up blood yesterday after my fall.

I know that bad things happen but I also know that good always comes from the bad. Something good will come out of this, I just know it. I know that I will be able to get back up once again, for I refuse to allow my injury to knock me down.

A lot of people get hurt and are able to get back up. If they can do it then I can do it too. I am no different. If I can no longer race I want to at least be able to ski again. For if I cannot then I will be lost. There is no choice. I have to ski. I have to get back up.

My dad always told me that success comes with hard work. I know that if I work hard then I will succeed. No one fails if they try.

I want to get back up more than anything. Skiing is something my entire family does. We all love this sport. My grandfather was in the 10th mountain division and he taught my dad to ski. My dad then taught me and Austin to ski. My mom learned how to ski at 19 years old. Our family is built around this sport. I have to get up and ski again. Quitting is not an option for me.

I know that it will be a lot of work and extremely challenging. I am up for the challenge though. Hard work brings success and success is what I aim to achieve. I know I can race again, just know it. I am strong and will get back up next season.

Surgery

I was ready to get surgery over with. Since my ACL wasn't a full tear, they only had to scope my knee. It was a Tuesday afternoon. I was in Swedish Medical Center in Denver. I had just gotten my gown on. It was really cold in the room that I was in, and I started shivering. My skin turned white with goose bumps.

The nurses brought me warm blankets. The blankets didn't help much. They kept bringing warm blankets to me. Each time the blanket that was wrapped around me cooled off, they would wrap another blanket around me. I didn't warm up, and my shivers got worse. They took about half an hour to warm me up.

They then gave me something to drink. It was really gross. The stuff tasted like a bad, sour, lemon (yuck). After I drank that nasty stuff, they put an IV in my arm. The IV was hard to get in because they couldn't find a vein. The goose bumps on my arms also made it hard to find a vein.

After they finally got the IV in, they allowed my mom to give me her sweater. I was still freezing. I was only able to put my right arm through my mom's sweater because my left arm had the IV.

A few minutes later, the anistiologisgt came in and put the cold sleeping stuff in me. After that stuff was in me, I had to take off my mom's warm sweater.

They wheeled me into the operating room. Already, I was starting to feel extremely sleepy. I was helped onto a cold metal table. Then I got the relief of going to sleep.

When I woke up, I had a tube in my mouth. The doctor told me to relax, and quickly took it out. When I was fully awake, my mom came in. She told me that I was able to come home. I was so happy. I didn't want to be in a hospital overnight.

The drive home from the hospital was fun. I got many calls from family. I enjoyed talking to my grandparents, aunts, and uncles. I rarely get to talk to them. It was real cool and thoughtful of them to call and check up on me. I also got to listen to my favorite music. That was fun.

When I got home, I went straight to bed. I was so tired. It felt good to be able to sleep with no one bugging me, or touching me. I had my room all to myself.

A few hours later when I woke up, my mom was walking up to my room to check on me. She had a bowl of chicken noodle soup. I ate that soup in two bites. I then decided that I was ready to walk around a bit. I got up out of bed and walked downstairs to where my dad and Austin were. They were surprised that I wasn't using my crutches. I don't like crutches. I don't use them if I don't have to. I had so many pain pills in me that I couldn't feel anything anyway.

My dad and I started talking about skiing. I told my dad that my goal was to get back up as a recreational skier next season. He and I both knew that my competitive days were over. I was upset by the fact that I wouldn't be able to race again. I was really hoping that I could make it to a college ski team, but I understood that it was going to be extremely hard to get back up on the course. I had to come to a reality that I wasn't going to be a competitive skier anymore. I knew that I somehow had to find a way to get back up, but I didn't know if it was even possible for me.

Journal entry

Dear Diary,

I had surgery today and I am extremely tired. My knee is throbbing as well. I am on a lot of pain medications but they do not seem to be helping.

It is kind of weird that I can even write, for the meds are making my brain foggy. I want to get back up on skis so bad. I really want to race again. I need to race again.

The ski season is now over, so I have all summer to relax and get better. During the summer I am going to work really hard and do what I need to do to get back on the course. More than anything I want to race. More than anything I want to get back up.

I want to be an Olympic gold medalist. I want to compete in the Olympics for my grandfather, who is the reason all of my family ski. I want to win the gold for him and let him be the first one out of the family to hold it. I want my grandfather to see me race in the Olympics.

More than anything I want to ski again. I can still feel the skis bend under my feet as I put them on edge. I can feel the snow grasp to the ski as I allow gravity to pull me down. I can feel the wind on my face and the wind blow my jacket. I need to get back up and race again.

I am in too much pain to write anymore. My knee is literally throbbing. It feels like my heart is in it. My eyes are tearing up and blurry, making my writing impossible to read. I do not know if I am crying more from pain or more of not being able to race again.

Working hard to get back up

Soon I came to realize that I had to get back up on the course. I new exactly what I had to do, and nothing was going to hold me back.

Every day, I would work hard to try to get strong again. Since I wasn't able to run, I would walk up and down my stairs until my knee couldn't take it anymore. I stretched it several times a day, every day. I used a ton of ice, and took anti-inflammatory for the swelling.

A month had gone by. I had been working so hard to try to get back up on skies. All I wanted was to be able to ski again. My knee was still extremely painful, and I still had trouble breathing at times because of my lung. Despite all the pain, I still found strength to keep going. I started going to church more. I prayed every night. I found strength in God. I couldn't have done what I did without God.

As the days went by, I got stronger and stronger. I soon realized that I was going to be able to get back up on skies. I felt much better too. My knee and lung were finally healing. I decided to push myself a little harder. I didn't just want to get back up on skies again; I wanted to race again too.

I was determined to get back up on the race course. I decided that the only way to do that was to work hard. The next day was Saturday. I got up out of bed, and ran on my treadmill for the first time since the accident. I was only able to run about half a mile. It took me eight minutes to run it. I was a little mad at myself for not being able to run further, or faster. I realized that I was recovering from a bad injury, and it would take time. The promise I made to myself that day was to never give up. I still keep that promise today.

The days went by quickly. I was soon able to run a half mile in five minutes, then a full mile. It was hard for me to get to a mile, especially with a bad lung. Soon a mile turned to two. I also started to lift weights. Weight lifting was important because I needed to gain the muscles back that I lost during my hard part of recovery. I started running every day. I would lift weights every other day. I also started a diet. My diet consisted of only organic foods. I would try not to eat foods that had additives in them. By diet and exercise, I was able to lose all the weight I gained during recovery. I had been out for three months. I had put on 15 pounds. That's a lot. Today, I have lost 20 pounds.

I am not the type of person who sits around the house and feels sorry for myself. Yes, I was upset about the weight I had gained, but I wasn't going to let it get to me. I was going to do something about it. I worked hard to get to where I am today. It was the hardest thing that I have ever done. I don't regret a thing. Everything that I have done was worth it.

It was now November, seven months after my accident. It was Thanksgiving weekend. I was having dinner with my family when Austin asked me if I was going to ski with him tomorrow. I said "Yes." I also said, "I'll race you down the course tomorrow." I wasn't just getting back up on skies, but I was getting back up on the course. Austin told me that he was up for a race, and that he was going to beat me. I said back, "well, we'll see about that." We both smiled.

First Day Back

It was Thursday morning. I was ready to go with my ski clothes on and my skies in my hand. Like usual I had a smile on my face. Getting back out there was something I had always dreamed of after my accident. I wanted this day more than anything and finally it was here.

Imagine having something that you love more than anything taken away in an instant. How would you feel? You would probably feel depressed or at a loss. You might even think "what next?" That is how I felt. I felt like my whole world was upside down. I did not know what to do at first because my mind was spinning constantly. Then I realized that my world did not have to be like this forever. My world was a mess at the moment but it did not have to stay that way. I decided to try to do something about it. It is not good to sit around and feel sorry for yourself. Instead of moping around and not trying, I turned the impossible into a possible. I was so excited that I succeeded that I didn't know what to do with myself.

Now imaging working hard to get that one special thing back. You would feel excited. It is such a gratifying feeling of accomplishment when you achieve something like that. I believe that work gives you a purpose in life. When you work hard you will succeed.

Anyway, I got back up on the snow. That first run on the mountain was awesome. As I felt the feeling of my skis pulling me down the mountain a feeling of freedom came over me. The cold air hit my lungs as I flew down the slope and the snow guided me down the run.

I felt a feeling of accomplishment as I was skiing that first run. It was the best feeling in the world. The best part about this day was yet to come.

When I got to the course it was all set up and ready to run. I was so excited to run the course that I could not control myself. I was jumping around and smiling. I just couldn't wait. My teammates were all around me, joking with me and just having fun. Some of them were throwing snowballs and others were being serious and concentrating on the course. As for me, I was having a part in the snowball fight.

A few minutes later my coach told me that I was up. I quickly made my way over to the start. The course looked perfect. I just knew that this was going to be a great run. A great run it was. I had the run of my life. It was awesome. The snow was perfect. There was no fear in me. I wasn't afraid of falling again or almost dying. That morning I had said a little prayer to God asking him to keep me safe. It was weird praying for me. I don't usually do that. God did keep me safe that day. There were no falls. There was just perfect run after run after run. That first day back up was the best day of my life. I not only got back up on skies, I got back into competitive racing.

When I got home I cried. This time I knew why. I cried because I was so glad that I had made it back. I cried because I survived. The tears were happy tears. My mom cried too. My whole family was so happy for me. I didn't want it to be all about me though. It was also about my family. They were the ones who helped me get better. They helped me get back up on skies. My family did a lot for me. This Thanksgiving was for them. It was a time for me to thank them for all they did for me. They did a lot.

Never Give Up

To me, giving up is the easy way out. No one should give up. It doesn't matter what people think. If you give up, you are just losing a part of you that you didn't know you had. Nothing is easy. Everything that you want takes time. It won't happen over night. Believe me, I wish it did. There is good news. When you are done, you will feel great. I can't explain the feeling. Everyone feels different. Just don't give up.

When I was lying on that snow, I had a choice. I could have either gave up and gone with God, or I could have fought and stayed with my family. I chose to fight. It would have been easier to have given up. If I would have gone with God, I wouldn't have had to go through pain. I also wouldn't be here if I didn't fight. The pain was worth it to me. I wasn't ready to die.

See what I mean. Sometimes life throws a curveball at us. We can either try to hit that curveball, or we can let it fly right on by. The choice is up to you.

I also had the choice whether or not to get back up on skies. Since I love to ski, I chose to try to get back up. I hit the curveball. I not only got back up, I got back to racing. Now, I am in training for the Olympics. I don't know if I'm going to make it, but all I can do is try. I won't know unless I give it all my strength. I am willing to work hard to get to the Olympics. It will be hard, but I am ready to take the challenge.

Your dreams don't have to be as big as mine, If they are, great. Good luck. Everyone can succeed if they try. Take it step by step. One day when you wake up, you will notice a change. When that day comes, you will feel like you own the world. It is awesome. Also, have fun while working. Making dreams come true can be a blast, especially when you succeed. Turn your impossible into your possible.

Pictures

Breckenridge: I am in Breckenridge with my
mom and just relaxing.

Breckenridge: Race day

Racing For Quantum Sports Club: 15 years old

Another race that I competed in

I am about 15 years old here, several months before the accident

Aubrie at 18 years old wearing her U.S.
Ski Team sweater

I am at Beaver Creek and it is the night before my
first race of the season.

Quantum Sports Club: My teammates

Wolf Creek ski area: My best friend and I

Chelsey and I have been best friends since high school. I am in the red and she is in the gray.

College Ski Team: Go Skyhawks!

Clowning around in Walmart with Chelsey before
a day of skiing (I am the blonde)

Thank You

Thank You for reading my story. I think that everyone has the potential to achieve great things with their life. I hope that you will go on and try your hardest with everything that you do. Life is short. Enjoy it while it lasts. You never know when your time is up. Remember that if a 15 year old girl can almost lose her life and the sport she loves, and then get back up doing what she loves, then you can do whatever you want too.

My wish for you is that you take every challenge head on. I also hope that you don't have any regrets when your time is up. Live like it is your last day.

I would also like to thank my mom and dad for supporting me with everything I do. I love you so much. You mean the world to me. Thank you for not letting me give up. You know me too well. That's not a bad thing.

Mom, you kept me alive. I was thinking about you losing your first husband. I knew that you wouldn't be able to lose a child too. I am so lucky to have a great mom like you. You are my inspiration. I don't know what I could have done with out you.

Dad, Thank you for teaching me how to ski. I am so glad that you gave me this gift. I will hopefully be like you when I grow up. You kept me strong. You kept me tough. Thank You so much. I love you. I will always be your ski buddy.

Austin, I know that we fight once in a while. That doesn't mean that I do not love you. You are my brother. Nothing can change that. I am thankful that we have a great relationship. You have always been there for me. I will always be there for you when you need me.

To the rest of my family, I am so glad that I have you in my life. You are all great people. I do not know what I could have done without you. You are all special people. I am so thankful to have all of you in my life. I love you all.

YOUR ENTRIES

1) Your turn: Write about a tough time in your
    life. How did you overcome it?

_____

_____

_____

_____

_____

_____

_____

_____

_____

_____

_____

_____

_____

_____

_____

_____

_____

_____

_____

_____

_____

_____

2) Your turn: What do you like most about your life?

_____

_____

_____

_____

_____

_____

_____

_____

_____

_____

_____

_____

_____

_____

_____

_____

_____

_____

_____

3) Your turn: If you had one wish what would it be? How can you make your dreams come true?

_____

_____

_____

_____

_____

_____

_____

_____

_____

_____

_____

_____

_____

_____

_____

_____

_____

_____

_____

_____

_____

_____

4) Your turn: What makes you happy?

_____

_____

_____

_____

_____

_____

_____

_____

_____

_____

_____

_____

_____

_____

_____

_____

_____

_____

_____

_____

5) Your turn: If you could accomplish one thing what would it be?

_____

_____

_____

_____

_____

_____

_____

_____

_____

_____

_____

_____

_____

_____

_____

_____

_____

_____

_____